This workbook belongs to:

_____

I started this workbook on:

_____ / _____ / _____

Published in association with the literary agency of Wolgemuth & Wilson.

Art direction and cover design by Nicole Dougherty
Cover concept by Bryce Williamson
Interior design by Janelle Coury
Artwork © Ninterints / Creative Market

For bulk, special sales, or ministry purchases, please call 1-800-547-8979. Email: CustomerService@hhpbooks.com

This logo is a federally registered trademark of the Hawkins Children's LLC. Harvest House Publishers, Inc., is the exclusive licensee of this trademark.

Becoming a Gospel Mom

Copyright © 2024 by Emily A. Jensen and Laura Wifler
Published by Harvest House Publishers
Eugene, Oregon 97408
www.harvesthousepublishers.com

ISBN 978-0-7369-8856-8 (hardcover)

Printed in China

24 25 26 27 28 29 30 31 32 / RDS / 10 9 8 7 6 5 4 3 2 1

BECOMING A GOSPEL MOM

EMILY A. JENSEN & LAURA WIFLER

HARVEST HOUSE PUBLISHERS
EUGENE, OREGON

CONTENTS

A NOTE FROM
EMILY & LAURA

Dear friend,

When we hit the ground running in motherhood, we often discover that our ideas about what we'll be like and the reality of what we are like are two different things. It can take years to unravel all of our thoughts and emotions, ideals and aspirations, sins and strengths. It seems like things would be easier if we were just handed a playbook for motherhood so our success was defined and we knew all the right steps to get there. Though God has not given us a step-by-step guide to becoming a good mom, he has given us himself and the opportunity to be declared good through Christ. Even though this isn't always the answer we are looking for, it is the best one.

We know that learning how to apply the wisdom from God's Word and respond to his guidance in life is challenging and requires a lot of slowing down and hard thinking. It takes trial and error, false starts, mistakes, repentance, conversations with wise friends, time, and prayer. But we also know it's worth it. There's more freedom to be found in the boundaries God has given us to discover in his Word than if he handed us a step-by-step manual that we had to follow to a T. His way is so much better, even if it can feel arduous at times. We also know that the right help at the right time can give just the boost that's needed to keep us running on the path of obedience to God. And that's exactly why we've created this workbook.

This study, along with the related *Gospel Mom* book, is a compilation of all we've learned about applying the gospel to motherhood—all the questions we've asked, all the stones we've turned over. Though we are far from perfect, examining our hearts and motherhood journeys through the lens of these things has immensely helped us to learn to find joy, freedom, and rest in Christ and the moms he's made us to be—and we've put it all in here. Call it our manifesto. Our master class. Our Gospel Mom academy. This workbook and *Gospel Mom* are our brains on paper, and we cannot wait for you to go through this workbook and go on your own journey of gospel motherhood.

Here are some quick recommendations on how to use this study:

First, read a chapter of **Gospel Mom,** *and* **then** *complete the corresponding workbook chapter.* You'll find that the book and the workbook are closely linked, and you'll probably want to reference some of the things you read. Our hope is that this workbook will help you go deeper and apply everything you're reading in the book to your own life. While there might be a way to use this study on its own, we don't recommend it. The context of all we shared in *Gospel Mom* will be crucial to understanding and following each question and exercise.

Focus on being honest and vulnerable about where you are at and what you're struggling with. There are not always right answers to these questions. Some are open-ended and might require more time and thought. Motherhood is full of complexity and nuance. We don't want you to feel like you're being graded—this workbook is for *you.* Though God certainly knows your heart and sees all, this book never has to be shown to anyone else.

Complete each section with prayer. Prayer is a critical part of staying in communication with God and being in tune with the work he's doing. We hope you'll be talking with him often and asking him to reveal things to you as you work through this so that you'll come out the other side transformed.

Keep your Bible handy. While we wouldn't label this a full-blown Bible study, in places, it's pretty close. We will ask you to reference verses often and even to do some study on your own. Though we hope these guided questions will lead you to lots of applications, there are many spots where you'll need to do the work of sitting in the Word first.

Find a friend. There are several options for group work with *Gospel Mom* and this workbook. First, you could do a book study of *Gospel Mom* and meet with other moms to go through the discussion questions at the end of each chapter. You could also read *Gospel*

Mom with a group and work through these exercises on your own. Finally, you could find a close friend or small group of friends to embark on this journey with. The questions get very personal, so we'll leave this up to you.

Take your time. It would be nice if completing this workbook wrapped up every question you have about motherhood into a nice little bow, but it won't. There might be a section that you leave incomplete and come back to later. There might be sections that take a while to complete. That's okay! God will keep working in your heart long after you close this book.

Now it's time for you to lace up your mom sneakers and hit the ground running. Where those shoes hit the pavement are the areas in motherhood where God wants the gospel and your everyday life to meet. He wants you to walk in his ways right where you are. And we can't wait to see how he leads you.

Your mom friends,
Emily & Laura

THINGS ON
MY HEART

Jot down a few things that are on your heart in motherhood right now. What prayer requests do you have? What areas feel particularly challenging or worrisome? How do you hope to see God work in and through this book and workbook?

_____

_____

_____

_____

_____

_____

_____

_____

_____

_____

_____

_____

_____

_____

A PRAYER TO
START THE JOURNEY

*Trust in the LORD with all your heart, and do not lean on
your own understanding. In all your ways acknowledge
him, and he will make straight your paths.*

PROVERBS 3:5-6

*Write a prayer based on this verse, and include some of the things on your heart
as you embark on the journey of becoming a Gospel Mom.*

_____

_____

_____

_____

_____

_____

_____

_____

_____

_____

THE GOSPEL MOM FOUNDATION

A Gospel Mom...

Gains a new heart and a new nature with Christ's righteousness. You do good not to earn anything but because good has been done for you and you know you are capable of following and obeying God's commands.

Knows her mission and purpose. No matter your earthly accolades, you live a life sold out for Christ, displaying his goodness to the world around you and sharing the reason for the hope that you have.

Lives free from the punishment of sin yet still wrestles with its power. You won't be perfect, and you will struggle with this tension of a sin nature until you reach heaven's shores. You know God is in the business of redemption—nothing is too far gone or too bad for him to redeem.

Understands the realities of a broken earth and the hardship of life east of Eden. You know suffering and sorrow will be constant companions throughout your days on earth, and you don't expect life to always be easy.

Lives free from mom guilt. Because there is no condemnation for those who are in Christ and your sins are fully paid for, you don't have to suffer under the suffocating weight of mom guilt. If you're struggling, you can dig under the surface and uncover whether you're experiencing true conviction from the Holy Spirit or condemnation as you fail to meet your own or your culture's ideals.

Rejoices because nothing can separate her from the love of God. When you fail, you can tell God, repent, and keep trusting him. He isn't mad at you or disappointed. He loves you more than you can ever imagine. You know God promises to help you, through the guidance of his Word and his Spirit and other people around you.

Recognizes the battle is against the world, the flesh, and the devil—not other moms. You know the battle isn't really about methods, ideas, or opinions on motherhood but instead against the spiritual forces of evil. You know who the true enemy is, and you stand your ground.

Walks in freedom from fear. While you know there are many things you could fear in this life, ultimately you only fear the Lord and believe that he is in control of all things. You rest secure that it's not up to you to control every variable or to protect from all harm.

Trusts God to continue to grow and change her. You know you are sealed with the promise of the Holy Spirit who is living and active inside of you, growing you day by day into the likeness of Christ.

Sets her sight on eternity and the glory that awaits. You don't live for the immediate rewards of today in your marriage or kids, your bank account, or your circumstances. Your gaze is fixed on the person and work of Christ and what matters for eternity. You live with hope and a future.

INTRODUCTION

Regardless of where your pictures of motherhood come from, all moms want to know—*What kind of mom should I be? And what do I need to do to get there?* While it's tempting to look for quick answers and formulas, the reality is that we have to trust God and walk by faith. We need his wisdom to know what kind of mom to be in the life and circumstances he's given us.

In the book, we talk about how other moms sometimes shape our ideals in motherhood. We make our own handbook and formula based on the things we like or don't like about other moms and their methods. In this book, we're trying to help you be more self-aware of what types of things you're drawn to and why.

Fill in the table on the following page. Note the specific moms, methods, or lifestyles you are drawn to, and list the things you admire about those expressions of motherhood and the things you might not want to emulate. There is no right or wrong way to fill this out; just write down what the Lord brings to mind, and allow yourself to brainstorm and be creative.

MOMS
Who do you admire, and why? (You can list people you know or moms you see online who you admire.)

MOTHERHOOD METHODS
What parenting methods or techniques are you drawn to, and why?

MOM LIFESTYLES
What lifestyles or ways of living are you interested in, and why?

Based on what you wrote in these tables, how would you fill in this blank? *(Don't give the "Bible answer" yet! Even if you do love the Lord and want to center your life around the gospel, are you ever tempted to fill in this blank with something else?)*

I think of myself as a _____ **mom.**

What do you believe makes a good mom? Where do you think your definition comes from? (Again, not your "Bible answer.")

_____

_____

_____

> Deep down, it seems like if we can just find the right word to fill in the blank, it will shore up our wavering hearts and give us the assurance we need that we have measured up on the scoreboard...
>
> But here's the catch—no matter how much we try to model ourselves after a certain type of mom (or maybe we're the mom who just waffles as she tries to find her type at all), we'll never be able to execute it perfectly. We'll find that we fall short and can't keep up in certain areas. Or that life hands us trials, sorrows, and circumstances neither we nor the manual were expecting. We might find that for a time, we can hold it all together according to our cultural model, but that often leads to us becoming smug and judgmental moms who are convinced we've found the one right way of being good while everyone else is falling short. Eventually, all of us find that we're still not totally happy with the mom we are, and we're left longing and questioning...
>
> There is a word that can fill in the blank before *mom* and lead us into faithful parenting. And it's probably not the word you've been searching for.
>
> *GOSPEL MOM*, **INTRODUCTION**

Even though we haven't done a deep dive yet, in your own words, write your best summary of the gospel. You can do this in a few sentences, or define the words Creation, Fall, Redemption, *and* Consummation.

_____

_____

_____

_____

_____

_____

_____

When people use the word *gospel*, they can mean different things. For the purpose of this book and how we're framing motherhood, we're using the word *gospel* to represent the metanarrative of God's redemption story through Christ for his people. The story of the good news of Jesus Christ is all-encompassing, and it also impacts all of life. The grand story of redemption is the one that informs all of our other roles and decisions. The mnemonic CFRC (Creation, Fall, Redemption, Consummation) is the tool we use to help ourselves and other moms remember the high-level points of this narrative so we can more quickly consider how they apply. We were not the originators of this idea—it's been commonly used throughout church history in various traditions. We've learned from a wide variety of Christian authors and theologians over the years as we've developed our thinking about how CFRC interplays with our unique circumstances, personal conscience, and heart motivations.

GOSPEL MOM, INTRODUCTION

Do you already believe and agree with the gospel? Explain your answer.

GOSPEL MOM
SELF-ASSESSMENT

Even if you're not sure you believe the gospel yet, the fact that you're engaging with this workbook shows that God is at work in your life. We're all at different points in our faith walks, so answer according to where you are right now. Consider referring back to the Gospel Mom Foundation on page 14 to 15 as you craft your answers.

(Hint: We'll revisit this self-assessment again at the end of the book, so be as honest as you can here so you can see how the Lord grows you!)

How has the gospel impacted you as a person?

_____

_____

_____

_____

_____

_____

_____

_____

Right now, do you believe God has a good plan for your motherhood? Why, or why not?

_____

_____

_____

_____

_____

_____

_____

How would you define success in motherhood?

_____

_____

_____

_____

_____

_____

_____

How would you define what it means to glorify God in motherhood?

_____

_____

_____

_____

_____

_____

_____

Do you think God's plan for your life and decision-making in motherhood is confusing and impossible? Why, or why not?

_____

_____

_____

_____

_____

_____

If you need to make a decision in motherhood, how do you go about figuring it out?

_____

_____

_____

_____

_____

_____

_____

What specific dilemma or question are you facing right now in your motherhood that you hope this book will give you clarity on?

_____

_____

_____

_____

_____

As you look at your answers **on the previous page**, list a few areas where you'd like to grow as you read this book and work through these exercises.

_____

_____

_____

_____

_____

_____

_____

_____

_____

_____

Glance at the tables of contents in both Gospel Mom and in this workbook. Which sections are you most looking forward to reading, and why?

_____

_____

_____

_____

_____

_____

_____

_____

_____

_____

_____

_____

What do you think it would take for you to have joy and freedom in motherhood? Are there any areas you're specifically hoping to focus on?

_____

_____

_____

_____

_____

_____

_____

Which part of the Gospel Mom Foundation makes you most excited, and why? (Refer to pages 14 to 15 of the workbook.)

_____

_____

_____

_____

_____

_____

_____

> God doesn't give you a formula or a precise point-by-point, product-by-product guide for every minute decision in motherhood, but he does give you his Word, with all the instructions you need to know to walk wisely through your motherhood journey. God doesn't leave you to figure all of it out on your own. He gives you his Spirit (and the church) to empower, help, and guide you along the way.

GOSPEL MOM, INTRODUCTION

CHAPTER 1

CREATION

God's design for humanity has deep implications for the life of a mom. Knowing God's intention for how we should live not only gives us enormous freedom as moms but also helps us remember our purpose and find direction on how we should live. Let's dive into this topic together.

> The things that are best for us both now and in eternity are the things that God laid out in Scripture. He is a loving Father who wants to keep his children safe and near—to see them have abundant and thriving lives, full of joy and purpose. He's not a Father who draws arbitrary boundaries just to keep his children from having fun or getting the most out of life on this earth. God is good, he's the ultimate designer, and his design is always the best possible thing for our lives.
>
> *GOSPEL MOM*, CHAPTER 1

After reading the chapter, explain in your own words the reason why God's design is good for us to know and follow:

_____

_____

_____

_____

_____

Put It into Practice: Discovering God's Original Design

In this chapter, we talked about the "Book of Scripture" and the "Book of Nature." Let's delve into these two topics.

Book of Scripture (God's Word)

In the table below, we've selected some straightforward passages from different sections of Scripture so you can practice spotting God's design for life as revealed in his Word. Read the verse and write one or two implications of God's design for mankind based on the passage. *Gospel Mom* chapter 1 mentions some specific things to keep in mind when reading different parts of the Bible.

Observations about God's good design

Creation account: Genesis 1:26-27
IMPLICATION:

Observe Israel (Law and History): Deuteronomy 6:6-8
IMPLICATION:

Wisdom: Proverbs 3:5-6
IMPLICATION:

Prophets: Micah 6:8
IMPLICATION:

Gospels: John 14:27
IMPLICATION:

Early church: Hebrews 10:25
IMPLICATION:

The end (prophetic): Revelation 21:3
IMPLICATION:

Book of Nature (General Revelation)

In the following table, we wrote down various "areas of knowledge"—areas of life we can learn from in order to deepen our understanding of God's design. For practice purposes, we're using the topic of friendship. Fill out this table to get the hang of it. Then you can choose your own topic based on what's relevant in your life. In fact, we've given you more of these tables on the following pages that you can use in the future. As a note: It's okay to leave some of these blank. This aspect of understanding God's design is much more abstract. Some areas might be clearer to you than others, depending on your personal interests, relationships, and so on.

Area of knowledge: *Example: Friendship* / **Observations about God's design**

RELATIONSHIPS
What have you observed that makes a healthy friendship?

CHURCH HISTORY
What character qualities have you seen in historical church figures (missionaries, theologians) that show you what it looks like to live faithfully as a friend?

NATURE AND CREATION
What does the intricacy and diversity of God's creation teach you about friendship?

SCIENCE AND RESEARCH
What do science and research tell us about our natural wiring toward having friends and meaningful relationships?

REDEMPTION STORIES

What is a story that has taught you about friendship and what it means to be a good friend?

COUNSELING AND THERAPY

How do past friendship experiences impact the kind of friend you are today?

DOCTORS AND NATUROPATHS

What are the impacts on someone's health when they experience friendship?

ART

Can you think of a time when a painting, a song, a book, or a poem helped you understand something about friendship?

WISDOM FROM LEADERS AND MENTORS

What is some wisdom about friendship you've heard from a mentor or person of influence in your life?

RELATIONSHIPS
How can this affect the health of relationships?

CHURCH HISTORY
What character qualities have you seen in historical church figures that show you what it looks like to live faithfully in this area?

NATURE AND CREATION
What can creation teach you in this area?

SCIENCE AND RESEARCH
What do science and research tell us about this topic?

REDEMPTION STORIES
What is a story that has shown a way to live in redemption in this area of life?

COUNSELING AND THERAPY
How do past experiences impact the way you approach this topic today?

DOCTORS AND NATUROPATHS
What are the ways this can impact physical health?

ART
Can you think of a time when a painting, a song, a book, or a poem helped you better understand this?

WISDOM FROM LEADERS AND MENTORS
What is some relevant wisdom you've heard from a mentor or person of influence in your life?

RELATIONSHIPS
How can this affect the health of relationships?

CHURCH HISTORY
What character qualities have you seen in historical church figures that show you what it looks like to live faithfully in this area?

NATURE AND CREATION
What can creation teach you in this area?

SCIENCE AND RESEARCH
What do science and research tell us about this topic?

REDEMPTION STORIES
What is a story that has shown a way to live in redemption in this area of life?

COUNSELING AND THERAPY
How do past experiences impact the way you approach this topic today?

DOCTORS AND NATUROPATHS
What are the ways this can impact physical health?

ART
Can you think of a time when a painting, a song, a book, or a poem helped you better understand this?

WISDOM FROM LEADERS AND MENTORS
What is some relevant wisdom you've heard from a mentor or person of influence in your life?

> *An important note:* God's Word is rooted in a certain time and place, but the truths within are timeless. God didn't hold back anything he wanted to tell us in Scripture; the big ideas and principles are clear. So if he didn't make an issue abundantly clear in his Word, like the specific methods and means of living his will, then we don't need to get too worked up playing detective about God's detailed boundary lines in every area of modern life. As we are trying to understand what is right and good and true, we can pair a deep biblical grounding, led by the Holy Spirit, with life experience and learn more about God's design for his people in the many different times and places and with the many unique issues facing his people.
>
> ***GOSPEL MOM*, CHAPTER 1**

Apply It to Motherhood in General

Based on what you learned on pages 30 to 31 in the workbook, how can you apply what you've learned from the Book of Scripture (God's Word) about God's design for motherhood? (Example: I know God wants me to tell my children about him and pass his truth down to the next generation. I want to take intentional time each week to do that.)

Based on what you have learned from the Book of Nature (through the exercises on pages 32 to 37 of this workbook), how can your understanding of God's design for motherhood positively change the way you mother? (Example: Research on the importance of reading high-quality litera- ture at a young age helps me understand how God designed mankind to love language and learn through good stories. I hope to incorporate that into the way I mother my children.)

_____

_____

_____

_____

_____

_____

_____

_____

In what areas of motherhood is God's design most difficult for you to understand?

_____

_____

_____

_____

_____

_____

_____

_____

_____

_____

_____

In the table below, write a few aspects of God's design that feel obvious or black-and-white to you versus areas that seem less clear or more open to personal preference or circumstance.

In God's design for motherhood, this seems obvious	In God's design for motherhood, this seems less clear-cut
Example: I should teach my children about God.	*Example: Specifically how should I teach them about God: With daily devotions? Organically? Formally?*

Clarity about God's design seems to exist on a spectrum. Some things that are really important are also very clear in Scripture, like big ideas and principles. But other things, like specific methods or means, are less clear in Scripture.

Why do you think Scripture is clear on some things and less clear on others? How does this help moms from every era and culture live according to his ways?

_____

_____

_____

_____

_____

_____

_____

_____

_____

_____

Apply It to Your Motherhood:

Think of a scenario where you're having a hard time figuring out God's design in a specific area of motherhood. Maybe you're wondering what to do or prioritize, or you're struggling to make a decision. For example, you might be thinking about how to help your child stay in bed at night. "Helping my child stay in bed" is the scenario. The broad categories you might consider are "discipline" or "sleep." Write down this scenario and walk through the topic with the provided questions. We've included a few tables on the following pages so you can work through several different scenarios. For now, feel free to just go through this exercise one time. We've given you a few extra pages so that if you want to come back with other topics, you can. Feel free to cite Scriptures and "show your work"! It's okay for this to take some time.

Tip: Feel free to reference the Abide Method, in appendix E of Gospel Mom, *for Scripture study guidelines. When determining the topic to study, start as broad as possible.*

Scenario (Specific to Your Life): _____

Broad Category of God's Design in Scripture: _____

How did God originally intend or design this to be?

How would it function without sin and brokenness?

How does it reflect the beauty of who he is?

Where does Scripture address this topic and the ways God has designed it to flourish?

What principles, standards, or truths have remained for all people for all of time?

Scenario (Specific to Your Life): _____

Broad Category of God's Design in Scripture: _____

How did God originally intend or design this to be?

How would it function without sin and brokenness?

How does it reflect the beauty of who he is?

Where does Scripture address this topic and the ways God has designed it to flourish?

What principles, standards, or truths have remained for all people for all of time?

Scenario (Specific to Your Life): _____

Broad Category of God's Design in Scripture: _____

How did God originally intend or design this to be?

How would it function without sin and brokenness?

How does it reflect the beauty of who he is?

Where does Scripture address this topic and the ways God has designed it to flourish?

What principles, standards, or truths have remained for all people for all of time?

Scenario (Specific to Your Life): _____

Broad Category of God's Design in Scripture: _____

How did God originally intend or design this to be?

How would it function without sin and brokenness?

How does it reflect the beauty of who he is?

Where does Scripture address this topic and the ways God has designed it to flourish?

What principles, standards, or truths have remained for all people for all of time?

Scenario (Specific to Your Life): _____

Broad Category of God's Design in Scripture: _____

How did God originally intend or design this to be?

How would it function without sin and brokenness?

How does it reflect the beauty of who he is?

Where does Scripture address this topic and the ways God has designed it to flourish?

What principles, standards, or truths have remained for all people for all of time?

Scenario (Specific to Your Life): _____

Broad Category of God's Design in Scripture: _____

How did God originally intend or design this to be?

How would it function without sin and brokenness?

How does it reflect the beauty of who he is?

Where does Scripture address this topic and the ways God has designed it to flourish?

What principles, standards, or truths have remained for all people for all of time?

FALL

The Fall has far-reaching effects on our lives as moms, and it's important that we're able to identify its impacts. In the book, we talk through the Fall in four main categories: the effects of the Fall on our hearts, on our relationships, on the earth, and on our bodies. Let's dig deeper to see what we can learn.

> Just three chapters into the Bible, things take a serious turn. It feels like the middle of a fairy tale, where everything goes wrong and you don't quite know how the characters will be rescued by the hero.

GOSPEL MOM, CHAPTER 2

What Happened in the Fall?

After reading the chapter, summarize the Fall in your own words. (Feel free to also read Genesis 3!)

_____

_____

_____

_____

_____

_____

_____

_____

Put It into Practice: Understanding the Fall

In chapter 2, we discuss the four main categories of our life on earth that the Fall affects. There's no way we could cover all the Bible verses that touch on the Fall, but in the table below, we've rounded up a few. Read the verses listed, then write observations about the Fall and the way it impacts different areas of life on earth. Refer back to the book if you need more explanation.

Observations about the way the Fall affects...

OUR HEARTS

Romans 8:7

Matthew 15:18-19

Genesis 6:5

OUR RELATIONSHIPS

Genesis 3:12-13

Isaiah 59:2

1 John 3:14-15

THE EARTH

Genesis 3:17

Romans 8:21-22

Genesis 47:13

OUR BODIES

Genesis 2:17

2 Corinthians 4:16

Psalm 6:2

These are hard realities. As Gospel Moms, we long to live out God's design, but we have to grapple with the bad news in order to fully appreciate and understand the good news that's coming. It is okay and right to grieve the realities of the Fall. This life isn't the way it's supposed to be, and everything in you knows it.

GOSPEL MOM, CHAPTER 2

Apply It to Motherhood in General

Explain the difference between something that happens as a result of sin versus something that happens as a result of the Fall.

Review the discussion in chapter 2 of Gospel Mom *on the far-reaching effects of the Fall. How have you seen the Fall affect moms in your community? Try to list several examples, one in each category of effects of the Fall that we explore in the book. (Example: I have a friend whose basement flooded, I have a friend who experienced a miscarriage, and so on.)*

How has sin impacted what we call the "mommy wars"? (Review Gospel Mom chapter 2 on how sin breaks relationship.)

Let's look at a common topic in motherhood—breastfeeding—and run through an example. While you might be long past this stage, it still makes for great practice as an example. We listed some questions below so you can exercise seeing and writing down the ways the Fall might impact a mom in this area. You can also practice with another topic on your own that feels more relevant to you!

Scenario (Specific to Your Life): _Example: Breastfeeding_

Broad Category of God's Design in Scripture: _____

In what ways might the Fall impact a mother's ability to breastfeed (including those she has no control over)?

How might a mom's sin nature impact her view of breastfeeding, her view of herself throughout the process, and her decisions surrounding it?

In what ways might a mom sin against other moms as she reflects on her own experience of and perspective on breastfeeding?

Apply It to Your Motherhood:

Think of a scenario where you're having a hard time figuring out how the Fall is affecting a specific area of your motherhood. Maybe you're wondering if you're sinning in a certain area, or maybe you're wrestling with a deep grief and loss. Write down this scenario in the table below, and walk through that topic with these questions. Feel free to cite Scriptures and "show your work"! It's okay for this to take some time.

We've included a few tables so you can work through several different scenarios. For now, feel free to just go through this exercise one time. We've given you a few extra pages so that if you want to come back with other topics, you can.

Tip: Feel free to reference the Abide Method, in appendix E of Gospel Mom, *for Scripture study guidelines. When determining the topic to study, start as broad as possible.*

Scenario (Specific to Your Life): _____

Broad Category of God's Design in Scripture: _____

Where does Scripture address your scenario and how it deviates from God's design because of the Fall?

If applicable, is this something that results from the effects of the Fall on the earth or the body? And if so, have you acknowledged this?

If applicable, how might you need to repent of sin that has infiltrated your thoughts, words, or actions?

If applicable, how has sin led to hiding, shame, and broken relationships?

What are some of the realities of living life after the Fall that you need to acknowledge instead of fight against?

Scenario (Specific to Your Life): _____

Broad Category of God's Design in Scripture: _____

Where does Scripture address your scenario and how it deviates from God's design because of the Fall?

If applicable, is this something that results from the effects of the Fall on the earth or the body? And if so, have you acknowledged this?

If applicable, how might you need to repent of sin that has infiltrated your thoughts, words, or actions?

If applicable, how has sin led to hiding, shame, and broken relationships?

What are some of the realities of living life after the Fall that you need to acknowledge instead of fight against?

Scenario (Specific to Your Life): _____

Broad Category of God's Design in Scripture: _____

Where does Scripture address your scenario and how it deviates from God's design because of the Fall?

If applicable, is this something that results from the effects of the Fall on the earth or the body? And if so, have you acknowledged this?

If applicable, how might you need to repent of sin that has infiltrated your thoughts, words, or actions?

If applicable, how has sin led to hiding, shame, and broken relationships?

What are some of the realities of living life after the Fall that you need to acknowledge instead of fight against?

Scenario (Specific to Your Life): _____

Broad Category of God's Design in Scripture: _____

Where does Scripture address your scenario and how it deviates from God's design because of the Fall?

If applicable, is this something that results from the effects of the Fall on the earth or the body? And if so, have you acknowledged this?

If applicable, how might you need to repent of sin that has infiltrated your thoughts, words, or actions?

If applicable, how has sin led to hiding, shame, and broken relationships?

What are some of the realities of living life after the Fall that you need to acknowledge instead of fight against?

Scenario (Specific to Your Life): _____

Broad Category of God's Design in Scripture: _____

Where does Scripture address your scenario and how it deviates from God's design because of the Fall?

If applicable, is this something that results from the effects of the Fall on the earth or the body? And if so, have you acknowledged this?

If applicable, how might you need to repent of sin that has infiltrated your thoughts, words, or actions?

If applicable, how has sin led to hiding, shame, and broken relationships?

What are some of the realities of living life after the Fall that you need to acknowledge instead of fight against?

CHAPTER 3

REDEMPTION

Are you as thankful as we are to live in this part of the story? Redemption is one of our favorite parts of the gospel framework, where we remember that we're not alone as Gospel Moms and we always have hope and help at the ready. Let's work through the implications of redemption in the life of a Gospel Mom.

> We live in the Redemption part of the gospel framework, believing that God is working in and through the hard or sad things for his glory and we get to participate in it. Without the completed work of Christ to save us and all the implications of that salvation, we might still be able to learn about God's design and feel the weight of the Fall, but we'd be stuck in our own cliff-hanger—no hope, no resolution, no sequel, and no good news. Thankfully, that's not where God left us.
>
> *GOSPEL MOM*, **CHAPTER 3**

After reading chapter 3, explain redemption in your own words.

_____

_____

_____

_____

_____

_____

_____

Put It into Practice: Understanding Redemption

Truths about redemption: In your own words, describe how each truth impacts your life today. *(Hint: Read the list of implications in chapter 3, and see if you can apply one to your life!)*

TRUTH: *Jesus came to earth as a man.*
IMPLICATION:

TRUTH: *Jesus lived a perfect life.*
IMPLICATION:

TRUTH: *Jesus died as a sacrifice for sin.*
IMPLICATION:

TRUTH: *Jesus was buried in a tomb.*
IMPLICATION:

TRUTH: *Jesus was raised from the dead.*
IMPLICATION:

TRUTH: *Jesus ascended to heaven.*
IMPLICATION:

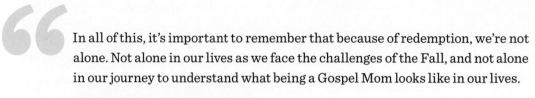

In all of this, it's important to remember that because of redemption, we're not alone. Not alone in our lives as we face the challenges of the Fall, and not alone in our journey to understand what being a Gospel Mom looks like in our lives.

GOSPEL MOM, CHAPTER 3

The Church

What role should the church play in a believer's life?

_____

_____

_____

_____

Apply It to Motherhood in General

Why does it matter that we understand where we are in the redemption story?

_____

_____

_____

_____

_____

Explain grace in your own words.

_____

_____

_____

_____

_____

In what ways do mothers try to earn their salvation instead of resting in the work of Christ on their behalf?

_____

_____

_____

_____

_____

How does being united with Christ secure a mom's identity no matter what happens to her in motherhood?

_____

_____

_____

_____

_____

What does it mean for a mom that she has the ability to go to God with anything and that he is real and active in her life?

_____

_____

_____

_____

_____

_____

Apply It to Your Motherhood:

Think of a scenario where you're having a hard time understanding how Christ is redeeming an area of your motherhood. Write down this scenario, and walk through it with the questions below. Feel free to cite Scriptures and "show your work"! It's okay for this to take some time.

We've included a few tables so you can work through several different scenarios. For now, feel free to just go through this exercise one time. We've given you a few extra pages so that if you want to come back with other topics, you can.

Tip: Feel free to reference the Abide Method, in appendix E of Gospel Mom, *for Scripture study guidelines. When determining the topic to study, start as broad as possible.*

Scenario (Specific to Your Life): _____

Broad Category in Scripture: _____

How can I look to Christ's example while he was on earth as a model on this topic?

Where does Scripture show how Christ has redeemed this topic?

How does knowing I am already eternally called "good" before God because of Christ free me to "do good" in this situation through the power of the Holy Spirit?

After thinking on the frameworks of Creation and Fall, in what areas do I see myself allowing lingering feelings of guilt and shame that God has not placed on me? In what areas is my guilt due to sin that I need to repent of?

Scenario (Specific to Your Life): _____

Broad Category in Scripture: _____

How can I look to Christ's example while he was on earth as a model on this topic?

Where does Scripture show how Christ has redeemed this topic?

How does knowing I am already eternally called "good" before God because of Christ free me to "do good" in this situation through the power of the Holy Spirit?

After thinking on the frameworks of Creation and Fall, in what areas do I see myself allowing lingering feelings of guilt and shame that God has not placed on me? In what areas is my guilt due to sin that I need to repent of?

Scenario (Specific to Your Life): _____

Broad Category in Scripture: _____

How can I look to Christ's example while he was on earth as a model on this topic?

Where does Scripture show how Christ has redeemed this topic?

How does knowing I am already eternally called "good" before God because of Christ free me to "do good" in this situation through the power of the Holy Spirit?

After thinking on the frameworks of Creation and Fall, in what areas do I see myself allowing lingering feelings of guilt and shame that God has not placed on me? In what areas is my guilt due to sin that I need to repent of?

Scenario (Specific to Your Life): _____

Broad Category in Scripture: _____

How can I look to Christ's example while he was on earth as a model on this topic?

Where does Scripture show how Christ has redeemed this topic?

How does knowing I am already eternally called "good" before God because of Christ free me to "do good" in this situation through the power of the Holy Spirit?

After thinking on the frameworks of Creation and Fall, in what areas do I see myself allowing lingering feelings of guilt and shame that God has not placed on me? In what areas is my guilt due to sin that I need to repent of?

Scenario (Specific to Your Life): _____

Broad Category in Scripture: _____

How can I look to Christ's example while he was on earth as a model on this topic?

Where does Scripture show how Christ has redeemed this topic?

How does knowing I am already eternally called "good" before God because of Christ free me to "do good" in this situation through the power of the Holy Spirit?

After thinking on the frameworks of Creation and Fall, in what areas do I see myself allowing lingering feelings of guilt and shame that God has not placed on me? In what areas is my guilt due to sin that I need to repent of?

CHAPTER 4

CONSUMMATION

The hope of God's plan coming to its ultimate completion is incredible to think about. While we don't know a lot of specifics, we do know enough to give us encouragement in the here and now. Everything is headed toward the finalization of God's plan, and we can trust in his promises. Let's explore this area of the gospel together.

Consummation means to finish something or make it perfect. When we talk about consummation in the gospel framework, we're referring to when Christ comes back for believers, judges all people, renews the earth, and brings his plan to completion.

After reading the chapter, explain consummation in your own words.

_____

_____

_____

_____

_____

_____

_____

_____

Put It into Practice: Understanding Consummation

Read each verse in the table below. Write down the truth about heaven the passage reveals, and then write down its implications for your life and motherhood today.

---

2 Peter 3:13

TRUTH:

IMPLICATION:

Revelation 21:27

TRUTH:

IMPLICATION:

Revelation 21:4

TRUTH:

IMPLICATION:

Mark 10:29-30

TRUTH:

IMPLICATION:

John 14:1-3

TRUTH:

IMPLICATION:

Revelation 5:13

TRUTH:

IMPLICATION:

Isaiah 25:6

TRUTH:

IMPLICATION:

Luke 12:37

TRUTH:

IMPLICATION:

Psalm 16:11

TRUTH:

IMPLICATION:

> And that leads us to the natural next question we have as Gospel Moms: *How can these insights about heaven change my thinking here and now? How can they help me press on toward heaven and seek the things above?*
>
> **GOSPEL MOM, CHAPTER 4**

Apply It to Motherhood in General

What things might make a Gospel Mom feel like an "alien and sojourner" (1 Peter 2:11) in this life?

In your own words, describe what it means to have a holy discontent. How can a mom be faithful and content with where God has her today while also longing for heaven?

Looking at the list of the implications of consummation for a Gospel Mom's life today, which one excites you the most, and why?

_____

_____

_____

_____

_____

_____

_____

_____

How might the reality of heaven change a mom's attitude and actions in her life today?

_____

_____

_____

_____

_____

_____

_____

_____

_____

Apply It to Your Motherhood:

Think of a scenario where you need hope and encouragement that there is a better life to come. Maybe you have a specific area of lack or suffering. Write down your scenario, and consider how these questions can help you find the hope of heaven.

We've included a few tables so you can work through several different scenarios. For now, feel free to just go through this exercise one time. We've given you a few extra pages so that if you want to come back with other topics, you can.

Tip: Feel free to reference the Abide Method, in appendix E of Gospel Mom, *for Scripture study guidelines. When determining the topic to study, start as broad as possible.*

Scenario (Specific to Your Life): _____

Broad Category in Scripture: _____

How does the assurance of future hope in eternity change my perspective and give me a purpose and mission today in the midst of my suffering?

How can I see that God is working for my greatest good in this situation, knowing he is sovereign and I am part of the greater story he is writing?

In what ways can I see that I am growing newer even while my body grows older?

Knowing I have Jesus, what do I have to lose in this life?

What verses, songs, and truths can I repeat to anchor my hope in Christ through my ever-changing circumstances?

Someday Christ will perfectly administer all justice and make all things right. How can that give me comfort today?

Scenario (Specific to Your Life): _____

Broad Category in Scripture: _____

How does the assurance of future hope in eternity change my perspective and give me a purpose and mission today in the midst of my suffering?

How can I see that God is working for my greatest good in this situation, knowing he is sovereign and I am part of the greater story he is writing?

In what ways can I see that I am growing newer even while my body grows older?

Knowing I have Jesus, what do I have to lose in this life?

What verses, songs, and truths can I repeat to anchor my hope in Christ through my ever-changing circumstances?

Someday Christ will perfectly administer all justice and make all things right. How can that give me comfort today?

Scenario (Specific to Your Life): _____

Broad Category in Scripture: _____

How does the assurance of future hope in eternity change my perspective and give me a purpose and mission today in the midst of my suffering?

How can I see that God is working for my greatest good in this situation, knowing he is sovereign and I am part of the greater story he is writing?

In what ways can I see that I am growing newer even while my body grows older?

Knowing I have Jesus, what do I have to lose in this life?

What verses, songs, and truths can I repeat to anchor my hope in Christ through my ever-changing circumstances?

Someday Christ will perfectly administer all justice and make all things right. How can that give me comfort today?

CHAPTER 5

SPIRITUAL DISCIPLINES

In part 2 of *Gospel Mom*, we learn that though we're saved by grace alone, through faith alone, God has designed us to grow healthy and mature through certain disciplines and habits.

> If we are like a plant, spiritual disciplines are like the stake we grow on... unsupported plants have the tendency to sag and bend toward the ground, becoming stunted and unhealthy. This is much like our faith...Without the stake or trellis of regular spiritual disciplines, our growth might stagnate. We might lose focus on the light of Christ and start to bend toward other things. Spiritual disciplines are regular practices that help us lean toward the light, stay committed to Christ, and create ripe conditions for maturity and good fruit. They help us stay tethered to God and his Word through every season.

GOSPEL MOM,
SPIRITUAL DISCIPLINES AND HABITS

Learning from Christ happens by the power of the Spirit, through action and intentionality on our part. It's like any other relationship we value and care about—as we make deposits on a regular basis, the relationship grows strong.

Spiritual disciplines should be fixtures in our lives, even though the amount of time we spend on each of them might vary depending on our season of life. Let's do an assessment of your spiritual disciplines and talk about how you might better connect your life to the Word of God.

What words would you use to describe your spiritual life right now?

_____

_____

_____

_____

_____

_____

_____

Why did you use these words?

_____

_____

_____

_____

_____

_____

Do you feel like your years as a mom are "lost years" in terms of spiritual disciplines? If so, why?

_____

_____

_____

_____

_____

_____

Taking inventory of your life right now, what are the four things you give the most free time to?

_____

_____

_____

_____

_____

_____

Which of the things you listed in the question above add value to your life, and which of these might you need to put more boundaries on in order to spend more time with Jesus?

_____

_____

_____

_____

_____

The Importance of God's Word

Read the verses in the table below. Based on what you read, explain why it matters to regularly abide in God's Word.

Isaiah 40:8
WHY IT MATTERS:

Proverbs 30:5
WHY IT MATTERS:

2 Timothy 3:16-17
WHY IT MATTERS:

Hebrews 4:12
WHY IT MATTERS:

Psalm 119:11

WHY IT MATTERS:

Psalm 119:105

WHY IT MATTERS:

Psalm 119:30

WHY IT MATTERS:

---

1 Thessalonians 2:13

WHY IT MATTERS:

Making Spiritual Deposits: The Practice of Spiritual Disciplines

In the chapter, we outlined several ways a Gospel Mom can stake herself to God's Word through the practice of regular spiritual disciplines. Using the following table, review the ways listed in the chapter, reflect on why these can be helpful, and consider how you are integrating them into your own life. We've left several blank spots to include spiritual disciplines that we didn't cover in depth in this chapter.

	How does this help a Christian grow?	How am I practicing this spiritual discipline right now?	How would I like to grow in this practice going forward?
Reading the Bible			
Studying the Bible			
Meditating on the Bible			

	How does this help a Christian grow?	How am I practicing this spiritual discipline right now?	How would I like to grow in this practice going forward?
Praying			
Church involvement			

Where do you look for truth and information about motherhood? What are the common websites, books, podcasts, and so on that you go to for answers? Who are the people you frequently seek out when you have questions?

_____

_____

_____

_____

_____

_____

_____

_____

_____

How can the regular practice of spiritual disciplines, like time in the Word and prayer, prepare you to discern and filter their advice through the truth of Scripture?

_____

_____

_____

_____

_____

_____

_____

_____

_____

_____

Look Outward

Remember, Gospel Moms don't live in isolation; they live in community. How could your regular spiritual disciplines and knowledge of the Word help serve and encourage others?

Other moms at your church: _____

_____

_____

Your husband: _____

_____

_____

Your children: _____

_____

_____

Your nonbelieving friends and neighbors: _____

_____

_____

Based on what you've learned in this chapter and the ways you'd like to use spiritual disciplines to grow in your life and impact others, write a prayer for God to help you in this endeavor. Consider using the ACTS method! (See *Gospel Mom* chapter 5.)

_____

_____

_____

_____

_____

_____

CHAPTER 6

SPIRITUAL HABITS

Spiritual formation is how we move our faith from our head to our heart. Apprenticing under Jesus means that we take what we're learning in God's Word and seek to implement it through our daily habits, rhythms, and practices.

> As we've cared for the plants in our own homes, we've discovered that each plant has common yet unique needs for flourishing. They all need some level of light, water, and nutrition—but when and how much? That's a whole different question! We've had to learn each plant's unique needs—how frequently it needs water, how much sun or shade it can handle during each season of the year, and when and how much it needs to be fertilized or pruned. In the same way that plants need regular care, we need regular rhythms of soul care to help us thrive and flourish.
>
> *GOSPEL MOM,*
> **SPIRITUAL DISCIPLINES AND HABITS**

Evaluating Our Spiritual Habits

In the chapter, we talked about five practices we see lead to a flourishing life: the habit of curation, the habit of friendship, the habit of nature, the habit of rest, and the habit of care. On the following pages, we're going to work through each habit in more depth and see how they matter to your gospel motherhood.

The Habit of Curation

Do you curate the media you consume? If so, what are your filters?

_____

_____

_____

What are signs that you need to eliminate or place boundaries on a type of media? (Examples: How much time you spend on social media; how a specific influencer, audiobook, or news source is impacting your patience, peace, and emotional energy for others.)

_____

_____

_____

♥ HEART CHECK

What are the main media sources you consume right now? (Examples: How much time you spend on social media; how a specific influencer, audiobook, or news source is impacting your patience, peace, and emotional energy for others.)

_____

_____

_____

_____

Habit of Curation

Pick one TV show, social media platform, book, or podcast that you consume on a regular basis, and use it to address the prompts in the table below.

My Curation Focus: _____

Does this media help me love God more?

Does this media treat humans with dignity and respect as image bearers of God (even if it is showing the complexity of the human experience and emotion)?

Does this media shape my emotions in a way that I can't sleep or function well in daily life?

Am I using this media as a distraction or a way to check out from my real-life responsibilities?

Can I give up this media entirely and still find happiness and joy in life and, ultimately, in Christ?

After completing questions above, do you think this is a media source that the Spirit is leading you to stop or change your engagement with? If so, what actions can you take? (Remember: Very few media sources will feel like they "pass" this litmus test. That doesn't mean we can't consume them, but it does mean we need to engage with them cautiously and wisely, being willing to forgo them if they become stumbling blocks.)

_____

_____

_____

_____

_____

The Habit of Friendship

Do you feel lonely in your motherhood journey? If so, what makes you feel so isolated?

_____

_____

_____

_____

_____

Where do you tend to source your friendships in motherhood? How many of these are found and fostered online or through social media versus in your real-life community? What are the pros and cons of each, and how might pursuing in-person friendships with other Christians improve the quality of your friendships and combat loneliness?

_____

_____

_____

_____

_____

♥ HEART CHECK

Who are some believing women with whom you are pursuing friendships right now? In what ways are these women good gospel friends to you?

_____

_____

_____

_____

Habit of Friendship

Answer the questions in the table below to think about how you can "become the friend you would want to have." We hope this helps you think about the ways you are displaying gospel friendship and investing in your relationships and connections.

What are my expectations for what a friendship can do and be in my life?
In what ways do I ask good questions and listen to my friends' responses?
In what ways am I vulnerable in relationships?
In what ways do I celebrate and share in my friends' joys and sorrows?

After looking at what makes a good gospel friend, are there any areas where you hope to change or grow? If so, what actions can you take?

_____

_____

_____

_____

_____

_____

What steps can you take to nurture a friendship with a believing mom?

_____

_____

_____

_____

_____

_____

No matter where you are in your friendships with other moms, in what ways has Christ been a friend to you?

_____

_____

_____

_____

_____

_____

The Habit of Nature

Before answering these questions, consider taking a few (focused!) minutes to do some online research about the ways going outside can benefit you and how the lack of it can be a detriment. Have you ever considered the value of going outside into nature to help you reorient your mind around the things of God? How can spending time outside help your mental, physical, and spiritual health?

Mental: _____

_____

_____

_____

_____

_____

Physical: _____

_____

_____

_____

_____

_____

Spiritual: _____

_____

_____

_____

_____

_____

_____

What do you notice about yourself when you're inside all day or don't have time to get fresh air?

_____

_____

_____

_____

_____

_____

Write down ways you can involve your family in experiencing the habit of nature. (Hint: There are several examples listed in the chapter!)

_____

_____

_____

_____

_____

_____

HEART CHECK

How can you use your moments out in nature to show your family the awe of God and his power and might?

_____

_____

_____

_____

_____

_____

The Habit of Rest

In what ways are you in need of rest?

_____

_____

_____

_____

_____

Do you believe that God wants you to rest and that he provides a way for you to do so in the midst of motherhood? Why or why not?

_____

_____

_____

_____

_____

How is God's plan and desire for your rest seen in his creation of the Sabbath?

_____

_____

_____

_____

_____

Looking at the examples and tips for practicing rest in the book, what are some ways you can implement Sabbath rest in your own life? What are you willing to let go so that you can experience rest?

_____

_____

_____

_____

_____

_____

The Habit of Care

When considering self-care, mark where you fall on the following scale.

I put my
needs last
on the list.

My needs
come first.

How did you determine where to put the mark on the scale? Based on what you read in the chapter, do you think this is a biblical view of self-care?

_____

_____

_____

_____

_____

How could caring for yourself in the following areas allow you to better care for others?

EXERCISE:

SLEEP:

NUTRITION:

FRIENDSHIPS:

SOLITUDE:

COUNSEL:

Knowing that you probably won't be able to focus on all of these areas at once, put a star by one area from the list above that you'd like to prioritize.

♡ HEART CHECK

Sometimes we're in seasons when we need to lay many of our needs down for others. What does it look like to depend on the Lord and live according to his direction even when you're not able to do these things as much as you'd like on a regular basis? Or how have you seen God provide and care for you when you weren't able to care for yourself?

_____

_____

_____

_____

_____

_____

_____

_____

_____

_____

_____

_____

_____

_____

"

These habits are...to cultivate a sustainable life for a mom who wants to follow Jesus until the end of her days. She doesn't have to do them; she *gets* to do them. They are the still waters and pleasant boundary lines of the abundant life.

GOSPEL MOM, **CHAPTER 6**

"

UNIQUE CIRCUMSTANCES

In chapter 7 of *Gospel Mom*, we took time to consider the many different factors that make each mom unique, and we started to explore how those factors shape the way she's going to apply the gospel and live out the motherhood God has given her.

> When we think about all that God has for us in motherhood, we need an understanding and appreciation of both the ways he's called us to the same mission and the ways he's leading us to live that out differently. Understanding how God's Word and the gospel come to bear on our lives is what biblical wisdom and decision-making are all about. And this starts by looking at and thinking about our unique circumstances. What are the facts of our situation—the realities about who we are, where we live, and what needs and resources we have available? How do we ask not just *What has God given her?* but also *What has God given me?*
>
> **GOSPEL MOM, CHAPTER 7**

Life Landscape

Let's zoom out and consider your unique circumstances in the life and mother-hood God has given you today (see *Gospel Mom* chapter 7 for more on this). Fill in each space with a few details. This will help you get your bearings on these broad categories as we dig deeper into the chapter.

MY HOME

_____

MY FAMILY MAKEUP

_____

MY TESTIMONY

_____

MY HOBBIES

_____

MY GIFTS

MY LIMITATIONS

MY WORK

MY CHURCH INVOLVEMENT

MY PASSION AREAS

MY RESOURCES

MY PERSONALITY

Unique Circumstances Questionnaire

Take a few moments to dig deeper by filling out these questions. The point of this exercise is to help you continue to assess the life God has given you. Don't get too bogged down with wordy answers! Use quick references just so that you know how these areas impact you.

How many years have you been a believer, and what is your personal journey of faith and your testimony of Jesus's work in your life?

What is your personal experience with church or Christian culture?

What was your journey to motherhood? *(Reference the book for more prompts.)*

Describe your relationship with your own mom and dad.

What aspects of your childhood were healthy, and what are things you don't want to repeat?

Describe your current physical health.

Describe your current mental health.

What are your particular habitual temptations or struggles?

Are you married? If so, is he a believer and/or how strong is his relationship with God?

How many children do you have? Do any of them have unique challenges?

What types of support or resources as a mom do you have available to you?

What type of community do you live in?

How do you spend your days?

What is your financial situation?

Are you a caregiver beyond your children? What does that look like?

What are your personal interests or hobbies?

Do you have certain areas of knowledge or life experience?

Where do you give your time, money, and attention?

Do you have any topics that you care deeply about?

What season of life are you in?

Evaluate

Go back to the introduction section of the workbook on page 19, and look at your answer for what you believe "makes a good mom."

How do the actual life landscape and unique circumstances God has given you in motherhood fit with your definition of success in motherhood? Is it realistic for you to obtain? Why or why not?

_____

_____

_____

_____

_____

_____

_____

In what ways are you aspiring to a life that is not yours?

_____

_____

_____

_____

_____

_____

_____

_____

_____

_____

_____

We can acknowledge our hopes and desires for the way we thought things would be but evaluate and accept the life that God has actually given us, the place we actually live, and the family we actually have. We don't live in the "what-ifs." We live our motherhood in the "what is."

GOSPEL MOM, CHAPTER 7

Have you come to terms with the life God has actually given you and the place you actually live, with the husband and family you actually have? Does anything need to change in order for you to live in the "what is" more fully?

_____

_____

_____

_____

_____

_____

_____

Apply It to Your Motherhood:

You've seen an overview of your unique circumstances in the form of a table and a questionnaire. Now let's dive into specific areas of your motherhood and start to see how your desires for motherhood can conflict with the life God actually gave you. Learning to think about how these realities affect your decisions is what it looks like to walk in wisdom.

When we don't acknowledge or accept our family circumstances, we can end up feeling unfounded guilt and condemnation about the things we need to do to care for our families. In the chart on the next page, write down ways that you have not accommodated the motherhood that God has given you, and reframe it through a lens of truth that acknowledges your realities.

Learning to live in the "what is" of _Example: birthday celebrations_

Life landscape category: _My family makeup_

Unique circumstances

I was never raised to make a big deal about birthdays, and they don't feel very important to me.

Impacts on my decisions as a mom

Because I was not raised with birthdays as super important, I don't place much value on elaborate planning, gifts, or celebrations for my kids' birthdays.

Discouragement or challenge

I feel like I'm a bad mom because I don't make as big of a deal about birthdays as other moms. I wonder if this is okay or if I'm really failing my kids.

Truth

How I throw birthday parties is not a measure of my worth as a mom. While I can work on showing value to my children by making their day special, I don't have to measure up to cultural standards for birthdays.

Learning to live in the "what is" of _____

Life landscape category: _____

Unique circumstances

Impacts on my decisions as a mom

Discouragement or challenge
I feel...

Truth

Learning to live in the "what is" of _____

Life landscape category: _____

Unique circumstances

Impacts on my decisions as a mom

Discouragement or challenge
I feel...

Truth

Learning to live in the "what is" of _____

Life landscape category: _____

Unique circumstances

Impacts on my decisions as a mom

Discouragement or challenge
I feel...

Truth

Now that you've thought more about your unique circumstances and how they impact your motherhood, how does this change your perspective on other moms and the decisions they make? How do you feel when you discover other moms are not as passionate about some lifestyle choices, methods, and areas of motherhood as you are?

_____

_____

_____

_____

_____

_____

_____

_____

_____

_____

_____

_____

_____

_____

_____

Note: We're going to practice this more as the workbook goes on and put all the pieces together. This is just to get you started.

CHAPTER 8

PERSONAL CONSCIENCE

As moms, we can often wonder what the "most God-honoring" way to do something is—and that's a good thing! We should want to honor God with our decisions and actions. Part of that is learning to understand our personal conscience and the role it plays in the life of a Christian mom.

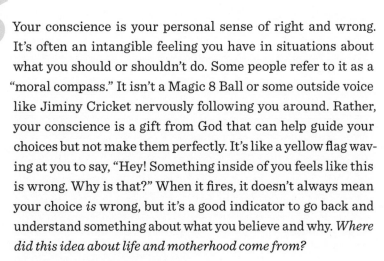

Your conscience is your personal sense of right and wrong. It's often an intangible feeling you have in situations about what you should or shouldn't do. Some people refer to it as a "moral compass." It isn't a Magic 8 Ball or some outside voice like Jiminy Cricket nervously following you around. Rather, your conscience is a gift from God that can help guide your choices but not make them perfectly. It's like a yellow flag waving at you to say, "Hey! Something inside of you feels like this is wrong. Why is that?" When it fires, it doesn't always mean your choice *is* wrong, but it's a good indicator to go back and understand something about what you believe and why. *Where did this idea about life and motherhood come from?*

GOSPEL MOM, CHAPTER 8

Assess Your Conscience

Looking back over your life, what are some of the major building blocks that have shaped your view of religion, politics, family roles, and success? In the chapter, we discuss how these views are shaped by things like family of origin, personal hurts or traumas, socioeconomic status, and more. We've selected a few areas for you to evaluate in your own life below.

Consider how the areas listed have impacted your current views and your definition of success. Fill in each blank with a sentence or a few phrases explaining the connection.

Family of origin

Politics:

Religion:

Family roles:

Definition of success:

Definition of a "good mom":

Personal hurts and traumas

Politics:

Religion:

Family roles:

Definition of success:

Definition of a "good mom":

Socioeconomic status

Politics:

Religion:

Family roles:

Definition of success:

Definition of a "good mom":

Education

Politics:

Religion:

Family roles:

Definition of success:

Definition of a "good mom":

Microculture you currently live in

Politics:

Religion:

Family roles:

Definition of success:

Definition of a "good mom":

Other:

Politics:

Religion:

Family roles:

Definition of success:

Definition of a "good mom":

After filling out this table, hopefully you can see how your views have been shaped by various aspects of your life and upbringing. What areas can you easily identify as having been more influenced by your life experiences than Scripture? Describe any new connections you perhaps haven't noticed before.

Troubleshooting Your Conscience

As moms, we long to make the best choices we can for our families, and that's a good thing! But it's important that we take our decisions, thoughts, and actions and submit them to God's Word and plan. All of us have areas where our conscience isn't aligned with God's Word, but sometimes it can feel hard to figure out what those areas are. We're going to go through some questions below to help you troubleshoot your conscience.

Do you have an overly sensitive conscience in a certain area? In the following exercise, think of an aspect of motherhood where you are strong and passionate that it's the "right" thing for a mom to do. One indicator that you feel strongly about something is if you saw a mom making a different decision in this area, it would cause you to feel anger, judgment, or frustration. As we wrote in the book,

> While it's good to have a tender and soft heart toward God and be sensitive to what he says is right and wrong, in some areas our consciences can be overly sensitive or hyperactive. We can start creating rules or laws that God's Word hasn't put in place and aren't universal for all of God's people....Those with a weak conscience tend to have a fearful or legalistic bent, putting themselves in the seat of judge and jury in areas where there is actually freedom in God's commands and laws.

***GOSPEL MOM*, CHAPTER 8**

Write your conviction on the line at the top of the chart, then answer the questions in the flowchart to evaluate the origins of your strongly held belief and what that means for your relationships with other moms. You might discover that your conviction is strongly based in Scripture, and you'll have to continue to bear with other moms as they grow and arrive at truth, or maybe you'll discover that this area was a bit more flexible than you previously thought. We encourage you to take a topic that you feel a strong conviction on that is divisive among believers in the church and can cause conflict, frustration, or fear. For example, don't use "I feel strongly that moms should pray."

For now, feel free to just go through this exercise one time. We've given you a few extra pages so that if you want to come back with other topics, you can.

I feel strongly that moms should / should not: _____

What helped form this strong conviction in your life? Is this a conviction you acquired over the years, brought on by personal experiences or cultural standards? *(Go back to the chart on pages 126 to 129 if you're getting stuck!)*

What good thing do you believe will happen if you adhere to this standard? In your opinion, what does it prove about you as a mom if you hold to this standard?

What are you afraid might happen if you don't hold to this conviction? In your opinion, what would it say about you as a mom?

Do you think this is a universal biblically supported truth that every mom should adhere to for all of time? (*What is your immediate reaction here? You'll get a chance to test this answer and think more about how it applies to moms in the questions below.*)

If YES...	If NO...
What are some specific Scripture references or principles that show it's commanded by God for all Christians?	What are your exceptions, and why?
What would it look like for you to be patient with other moms as they arrive at the truth?	If you believe there are exceptions, how do you treat another mom who is violating your standard?

I feel strongly that moms should / should not: _____

What helped form this strong conviction in your life? Is this a conviction you acquired over the years, brought on by personal experiences or cultural standards? *(Go back to the chart on pages 126 to 129 if you're getting stuck!)*

What good thing do you believe will happen if you adhere to this standard? In your opinion, what does it prove about you as a mom if you hold to this standard?

What are you afraid might happen if you don't hold to this conviction? In your opinion, what would it say about you as a mom?

Do you think this is a universal biblically supported truth that every mom should adhere to for all of time? (*What is your immediate reaction here? You'll get a chance to test this answer and think more about how it applies to moms in the questions below.*)

If YES...	If NO...
What are some specific Scripture references or principles that show it's commanded by God for all Christians?	What are your exceptions, and why?
What would it look like for you to be patient with other moms as they arrive at the truth?	If you believe there are exceptions, how do you treat another mom who is violating your standard?

I feel strongly that moms should / should not: _____

What helped form this strong conviction in your life? Is this a conviction you acquired over the years, brought on by personal experiences or cultural standards? (*Go back to the chart on pages 126 to 129 if you're getting stuck!*)

What good thing do you believe will happen if you adhere to this standard? In your opinion, what does it prove about you as a mom if you hold to this standard?

What are you afraid might happen if you don't hold to this conviction? In your opinion, what would it say about you as a mom?

Do you think this is a universal biblically supported truth that every mom should adhere to for all of time? (*What is your immediate reaction here? You'll get a chance to test this answer and think more about how it applies to moms in the questions below.*)

If YES...	**If NO...**
What are some specific Scripture references or principles that show it's commanded by God for all Christians?	What are your exceptions, and why?
What would it look like for you to be patient with other moms as they arrive at the truth?	If you believe there are exceptions, how do you treat another mom who is violating your standard?

HEART CHECK

Do you have a seared or dulled conscience in a certain area? In the following exercise, think of an aspect of motherhood where you used to feel conviction, but over time, your convictions have worn down, and you now feel laissez-faire about it. One indicator that your conscience is dulled is that you no longer feel sensitive to things that are impure or ungodly.

> A dull or seared conscience puts us in danger of falling into sinful habits and not actually feeling all that bad about it because the voice of our conscience has grown dim as we stuffed it down over and over again.
>
> ***GOSPEL MOM,* CHAPTER 8**

As you work through these questions, maybe you'll discover that you've veered off the path of obedience to God in an area of life and need to create new boundaries as you seek to walk in his ways again.

Our encouragement to you is to take something you remember feeling bad about the first time you did it (watching a show with nudity and explicit bedroom scenes, having a glass of wine each night, yelling at your children in impatience, gossiping, and so on) and consider why this has gotten easier or less "wrong" feeling over time. If you can't think of anything, pray and ask the Holy Spirit to bring something to mind.

*Note: Remember, the conscience is not the same thing as the Holy Spirit, so it's possible that you feel things are wrong that aren't biblically wrong. If you have an overly sensitive conscience, you might discover the reason you don't feel a yellow flag anymore in your conscience is because what you were doing was not actually wrong. Your conscience has actually been freed over time, as you're not holding as rigidly to extra biblical rules. This is **not the same thing** as a dulled or seared conscience. We will cover this in the next section.*

For now, feel free to just go through this exercise one time. We've given you a few extra pages so that if you want to come back with other topics, you can.

I used to feel conviction about: _____

Are there any areas of motherhood that are clearly sin that you have failed to correct?

What has made you comfortable with this and has kept you from repentance and fighting sin in this area of life?

What action might you take today to help sensitize you to that area again? *Tip: Write down one verse from Scripture below that pertains to the area you want to grow more sensitive to. Consider posting it in an area of your home you spend a lot of time in.*

I used to feel conviction about: _____

Are there any areas of motherhood that are clearly sin that you have failed to correct?

What has made you comfortable with this and has kept you from repentance and fighting sin in this area of life?

What action might you take today to help sensitize you to that area again? *Tip: Write down one verse from Scripture below that pertains to the area you want to grow more sensitive to. Consider posting it in an area of your home you spend a lot of time in.*

I used to feel conviction about: _____

Are there any areas of motherhood that are clearly sin that you have failed to correct?

What has made you comfortable with this and has kept you from repentance and fighting sin in this area of life?

What action might you take today to help sensitize you to that area again? *Tip: Write down one verse from Scripture below that pertains to the area you want to grow more sensitive to. Consider posting it in an area of your home you spend a lot of time in.*

Right now, you probably have many areas where your conscience does align with God, but all of us have areas where we might be hypersensitive or in sin that we'll continue to uncover throughout our lives. Chances are, if you've been a believer for a while, you might have noticed how God tends to reveal certain sins or proclivities in batches—not everything all at once. This is a kindness! If he were asking us to work on everything in every facet of life, we would be buried so deep we wouldn't be able to find a way out.

As with many things, once we have a good understanding of God's laws and commands, we'll find that we have freedom where God's Word hasn't given a clear directive—at the end of the day, in these "gray areas," the Lord is often more concerned with who we are and how we go about our decisions than what we specifically decide.

GOSPEL MOM, CHAPTER 8

Freeing Your Conscience

Based on the two activities you completed about an overly sensitive or a seared conscience, what are some ways that you can free your conscience to closer align to God's Word and design? As we wrote in the book, in God's kindness, our consciences can be freed or changed when we take time to understand why we think what we think or believe what we believe. Write down at least three specific things you can start to work on immediately. *Tip: If you're stuck, refer back to chapter 8 in the book, where we talk about freeing the conscience.*

1

2

3

Are there areas that you are currently still evaluating and trying to determine where your conscience lies? As we noted in the book, you shouldn't act on something if you have any doubts. What steps can you take today to become more "fully convinced in [your] own mind" of where God might be moving your conscience (Romans 14:5)?

♥ HEART CHECK

How can you live within your conscience? As we've noted, your conscience is not the same as the Holy Spirit, which means we are always growing and changing in our understanding of how to align our conscience with God's Word. Because we know motherhood is always filled with new decisions and adjustments, we've created a few heart check questions for you to work through in gray areas of motherhood that God has given you freedom in. Remember, the Lord is often more concerned with who we are and how we go about our decisions than what we specifically decide.

List a gray-area decision you are currently processing in motherhood based on your conscience and informed by God's Word:

_____

_____

Are you making this decision in faith? How are you trusting and looking to the Lord as you move forward in this?

_____

_____

_____

_____

What proof points can you write down to show you are operating with wisdom informed by God's Word rather than worldly wisdom?

_____

_____

_____

_____

_____

How are you reflecting Christ in this decision through your heart attitudes, words, and behaviors?

_____

_____

_____

_____

_____

_____

Have you considered how this decision might impact your Christian witness and ability to spread the gospel to others and love your neighbor?

_____

_____

_____

_____

_____

_____

_____

> Christ died for your pride, judgment, guilt, sin, and shame. He redeems you where you misstep in your decisions and feelings and frees you to walk as a new creation...Our goal should be to slowly but surely calibrate our consciences to become more and more in line with God's will and Word.

GOSPEL MOM, **CHAPTER 8**

HEART MOTIVATIONS

In chapter 9, we spent time looking at our heart motivations in motherhood—the "why" behind many of our decisions and actions. We discovered that we're often motivated by a deep desire to give our lives to something bigger than ourselves in exchange for something we want (namely, approval and knowing we're a good mom). If we don't evaluate who or what we actually give our hearts and lives to, we might miss the opportunity to worship and follow God himself.

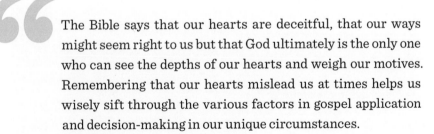

The Bible says that our hearts are deceitful, that our ways might seem right to us but that God ultimately is the only one who can see the depths of our hearts and weigh our motives. Remembering that our hearts mislead us at times helps us wisely sift through the various factors in gospel application and decision-making in our unique circumstances.

GOSPEL MOM, CHAPTER 9

Uncover: What Do I Really, Really Want? Why Do I Want This So Badly?

Think of an area of motherhood that you tend to pour your "all" into. Have you ever considered that it might be an area that you're worshipping? As we say in the book,

> Worship is an expression of our commitment to or our adoration of something or someone—it's spending our time, attention, care, words, and precious resources on what we love and value. When we worship, we bring figurative offerings and sacrifices to the altar of something or someone in our lives, and we lay those things down, typically in exchange for something we desire—unconditional love and acceptance, wealth, popularity, happiness, and so on.

GOSPEL MOM, **CHAPTER 9**

Go back to the question on page 19 in the introduction section of this workbook. What was the word that you put in the blank before *mom*?

Considering yourself a _____ **mom...**

What might you be worshipping? What sacrifices do you make in order to be that kind of mom?

_____

_____

_____

What are you hoping to get in exchange?

_____

_____

_____

_____

Knowing we are Gospel Moms,

Who do you worship? What do you need to sacrifice or lay down in order to worship fully?

_____

_____

_____

_____

_____

_____

What do you get in exchange?

_____

_____

_____

_____

_____

_____

"

Uncovering and tearing down our idols to reorient our worship toward God takes humility, compassion, and curiosity. It takes prayer and the leading of the Spirit, who searches and knows our hearts. It takes being willing to notice where our time and money and energy *actually* go versus where we think they go.

GOSPEL MOM, **CHAPTER 9**

"

Counting the Cost: Strategic Questions as You Consider a Decision

As we begin to understand what we worship and why we "do what we do" in motherhood, we also need to employ wisdom to count the cost of our decisions. We know how easy it is to move quickly in motherhood, but the gospel call is one to slow down and consider the risks and rewards, the pros and cons of our decisions, particularly in larger choices we're making. Counting the cost is a skill, and one that all Gospel Moms need.

In *Gospel Mom* chapter 9, the section on "counting the cost" includes several questions to help you make decisions. These questions have been used in the chart below. Take a decision or desire you have in motherhood and run it through the litmus test. *(Example: Should I let my child enroll in more than one activity at a time? Should I continue to dye my hair every six weeks?)* While it might not serve up the exact answer, it will help you evaluate the risks and rewards of your choices in an area that might feel unclear or muddy.

If you'd like more clarity about what we mean for the questions in the table, feel free to refer back to the chapter, where we offer a fuller explanation and more examples. For now, feel free to just go through this exercise one time. We've given you a few extra pages so that if you want to come back with other topics, you can.

Litmus Test for Decision/Desire: _____

What is the cost to me / our family? Is it worth it?

How does this align with my family's circumstances and values?

How permanent is this decision?

Can I be transparent about this decision? Why do I feel bad about this in some situations?

Litmus Test for Decision/Desire: _____

What is the cost to me / our family? Is it worth it?

How does this align with my family's circumstances and values?

How permanent is this decision?

Can I be transparent about this decision? Why do I feel bad about this in some situations?

Litmus Test for Decision/Desire: _____

What is the cost to me / our family? Is it worth it?

How does this align with my family's circumstances and values?

How permanent is this decision?

Can I be transparent about this decision? Why do I feel bad about this in some situations?

Litmus Test for Decision/Desire: _____

What is the cost to me / our family? Is it worth it?

How does this align with my family's circumstances and values?

How permanent is this decision?

Can I be transparent about this decision? Why do I feel bad about this in some situations?

Litmus Test for Decision/Desire: _____

What is the cost to me / our family? Is it worth it?

How does this align with my family's circumstances and values?

How permanent is this decision?

Can I be transparent about this decision? Why do I feel bad about this in some situations?

BUT WHAT DO WE DO ABOUT ALL THE OTHER MOMS?

In chapter 10, we faced the reality that not all Gospel Moms will make the same decisions and apply the gospel in the same ways. Each mom will use wisdom and follow the Lord's leading in her life according to her unique circumstances, personal conscience, and heart motivations. Sometimes, these differences are hard because we wonder if "different" means someone is getting it wrong. When our choices look different from those of our believing friends, we can doubt our own faithfulness or doubt theirs, sometimes before we've even asked good questions or considered the bigger picture at hand.

We walked through 1 Corinthians 10:23-33 to think through what it looks like to live in unity with and love other Christian moms as well as how we all apply the gospel in different ways. We've printed the whole text here for quick reference:

"All things are lawful," but not all things are helpful. "All things are lawful," but not all things build up. Let no one seek his own good, but the good of his neighbor. Eat whatever is sold in the meat market without raising any question on the ground of conscience. For "the earth is the Lord's, and the fullness thereof." If one of the unbelievers invites you to dinner and you are disposed to go, eat whatever is set before you without raising any question on the ground of conscience. But if someone says to you, "This has been offered in sacrifice," then do not eat it, for the sake of the one who informed you, and for the sake of conscience—I do not mean your conscience, but his. For why should my liberty be determined by someone else's conscience? If I partake with thankfulness, why am I denounced because of that for which I give thanks? So, whether you eat or drink, or whatever you do, do all to the glory of God. Give no offense to Jews or to Greeks or to the church of God, just as I try to please everyone in everything I do, not seeking my own advantage, but that of many, that they may be saved (1 Corinthians 10:23-33).

> Though we don't have much context for this debate in our modern faith, we are familiar with lots of other debates that Christian moms have—like whether or not you can have income-producing work outside of the home (and if so, how much), whether or not you ought to homeschool or pursue other school options, what you feed your kids, or how clean, natural, low-tech, holistic, and toxin-free your lifestyle is, just to name a few.
>
> *GOSPEL MOM*, CHAPTER 10

Let's take time to examine areas of motherhood where you can apply this passage to your life, church, and relationships.

🩶 HEART CHECK

Have you ever felt misunderstood or misjudged in motherhood? How did that make you feel?

_____

_____

_____

_____

On the flip side, when have you ever struggled to understand another mom's choice or felt like someone was taking an action or making a decision that felt contrary to yours? How did that make you feel?

_____

_____

_____

_____

In what ways are you striving to consider how your decisions impact other moms? (You can give examples from real life or your interactions on social media.) Are there quick areas that come to mind where you can show deference?

_____

_____

_____

_____

In the questions below, we will dig deeper into 1 Corinthians 10:23-33 like we did in chapter 10 of the book.

> 23 "All things are lawful," but not all things are helpful. "All things are lawful,"
> but not all things build up.

Think through a situation where you have a friend or family member who does something differ-ent from you. As Gospel Moms, we have tremendous freedom to live in different ways, but not all things build up the church or help others. Are there things that you have Christian freedom to do but shouldn't (for example, not allowing the video game console to be played when a friend's child is over who doesn't feel comfortable with video games)? Tip: If you can't think of anything, perhaps refer back to the chapter in the book for examples.

> 24 Let no one seek his own good, but the good of his neighbor.

Take a moment to consider a friend of yours who is in a tender place due to hardship, sorrow, or grief. In what ways are you laying down your own desires or freedoms in your relationship with her to show her that you seek her good?

32-33 Give no offense...I try to please everyone in everything I do, not seeking my own advantage, but that of many, that they may be saved.

Take a moment to reflect. What tends to motivate your family's decisions—comfort, ease, upward mobility, opportunity? What might change about your lifestyle if you considered how your family's choices and actions could be missional to spread the gospel and be a witness for Christ?

_____

_____

_____

_____

_____

_____

31 So, whether you eat or drink, or whatever you do, do all to the glory of God.

List two to three ways you can slow down in order to seek the unity of other moms you spend time with (online or off!). What are some ways you can think, act, or speak that show others the character and ways of God? Tip: If you need some ideas, refer back to chapter 10 of the book.

_____

_____

_____

_____

_____

_____

_____

List two to three ways you can stop to praise God for who he is and the work he's done in your life. Just like telling others about a great new deal you got, how can you spread the word about God's goodness, giving credit to him alone?

_____

_____

_____

_____

_____

List two to three ways you can show others that God is at the center of your attention and worship today.

_____

_____

_____

_____

_____

> As a Gospel Mom, you're seeking to humbly align your heart and actions with the Lord as you love those around you, not just make outwardly "good" choices with a heart of pride and self-sufficiency. Similarly, in gray-area decisions, it's important to care about the motives and heart posture of another mom and not just the choice she's making. This perspective puts God, his ways, and our hearts at the center of our focus, not just our choices and behaviors.

GOSPEL MOM, CHAPTER 10

When You're Not the Right Fit

On this side of heaven, we're not going to be perfectly unified with all believers, but that doesn't mean that we throw truth, love, and kindness out the window. Sometimes we're going to have to troubleshoot relationships, create boundaries, and be thoughtful about how much time and energy we can spend with another mom who does life differently than we do.

As you answer these questions, try to think of a specific Christian mom in your life whom you have struggled to get along with.

In what way have you placed yourself in the seat of judge and jury to determine if she is in or outside of God's will? What would it look like to get the log out of your own eye (Matthew 7:3) and approach this mom with humility and curiosity before making a judgment?

_____

_____

_____

_____

_____

_____

_____

_____

As you reflect on your relationship with this mom, do you think God might be calling you to bear with her in love and disciple her over time? If so, what would that look like?

_____

_____

_____

_____

_____

On the flip side, do you think God might be calling you to still show her love yet draw stronger personal boundaries? If so, what would that look like?

> Sometimes, we need a reminder that we don't have to be best friends with everyone. If there is a mom who you really don't align with on issues of personal conscience, and you can't see eye to eye or get to a point where you understand or respect where her conscience lies, you don't have to feel pressure to spend a lot of time with her. Perhaps her conscience is so firm on certain topics that she causes feelings of anxiety or fear each time you engage with her. Conversely, maybe you recognize that while you're trying to be sensitive, you can't censor your lifestyle from her completely to honor her boundaries. In these cases, you can still show her love and kindness when you interact with her and ensure that you speak about her with integrity and truth, but you don't have to be close friends with her if it is particularly challenging to maintain a relationship. If she sincerely follows Christ, trust that the Spirit is at work in her life and her family just as he is in yours.

GOSPEL MOM, CHAPTER 10

Take a moment to write down a prayer to ask God for direction in how to love this fellow mom well.

CHAPTER 11

WHAT KIND OF MOMS?

As you complete this workbook, we hope you've already observed some transformation, but we're getting ready to really take a look at how God is working in your heart. Remember that self-assessment you took at the beginning of the workbook? It's time to take it again, knowing all that you've learned about what it means to be a Gospel Mom.

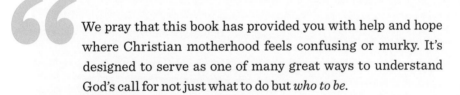

We pray that this book has provided you with help and hope where Christian motherhood feels confusing or murky. It's designed to serve as one of many great ways to understand God's call for not just what to do but *who to be.*

GOSPEL MOM, CHAPTER 11

GOSPEL MOM
SELF-ASSESSMENT

Please answer these questions, and then refer back to the self-assessment you took on pages 23 to 25 of this workbook to see how far you've come!

How has the gospel impacted you as a person?

_____

_____

_____

_____

_____

Right now, do you believe God has a good plan for your motherhood? Why, or why not?

_____

_____

_____

_____

_____

How would you define success in motherhood?

_____

_____

_____

_____

_____

How would you define what it means to glorify God in motherhood?

_____

_____

_____

_____

_____

_____

Do you think God's plan for your life and decision-making in motherhood is confusing and impossible? Why, or why not?

_____

_____

_____

_____

_____

_____

_____

If you need to make a decision in motherhood, how do you go about figuring it out?

_____

_____

_____

_____

_____

_____

Referring back to the specific dilemma or question you listed at the bottom of page 25 in the first self-assessment, what clarity did you receive?

_____

_____

_____

_____

_____

_____

List some areas you grew in as you read the book and completed the workbook.

_____

_____

_____

_____

_____

Which section of the workbook did you most enjoy, and why?

_____

_____

_____

_____

_____

_____

In what areas of motherhood have you found joy and freedom?

_____

_____

_____

_____

_____

_____

_____

_____

Which part of being a Gospel Mom makes you most excited? (See the Gospel Mom Foundation on the next page.)

_____

_____

_____

_____

_____

_____

_____

_____

_____

THE GOSPEL
MOM FOUNDATION

A Gospel Mom…

Gains a new heart and a new nature with Christ's righteousness. You do good not to earn anything but because good has been done for you and you know you are capable of following and obeying God's commands.

Knows her mission and purpose. No matter your earthly accolades, you live a life sold out for Christ, displaying his goodness to the world around you and sharing the reason for the hope that you have.

Lives free from the punishment of sin yet still wrestles with its power. You won't be perfect, and you will struggle with this tension of a sin nature until you reach heaven's shores. You know God is in the business of redemption—nothing is too far gone or too bad for him to redeem.

Understands the realities of a broken earth and the hardship of life east of Eden. You know suffering and sorrow will be constant companions throughout your days on earth, and you don't expect life to always be easy.

Lives free from mom guilt. Because there is no condemnation for those who are in Christ and your sins are fully paid for, you don't have to suffer under the suffocating weight of mom guilt. If you're struggling, you can dig under the surface and uncover whether you're experiencing true conviction from the Holy Spirit or condemnation as you fail to meet your own or your culture's ideals.

Rejoices because nothing can separate her from the love of God. When you fail, you can tell God, repent, and keep trusting him. He isn't mad at you or disappointed. He loves you more than you can ever imagine. You know God promises to help you, through the guidance of his Word and his Spirit and other people around you.

Recognizes the battle is against the world, the flesh, and the devil— not other moms. You know the battle isn't really about methods, ideas, or opinions on motherhood but instead against the spiritual forces of evil. You know who the true enemy is, and you stand your ground.

Walks in freedom from fear. While you know there are many things you could fear in this life, ultimately you only fear the Lord and believe that he is in control of all things. You rest secure that it's not up to you to control every variable or protect from all harm.

Trusts God to continue to grow and change her. You know you are sealed with the promise of the Holy Spirit who is living and active inside of you, growing you day by day into the likeness of Christ.

Sets her sight on eternity and the glory that awaits. You don't live for the immediate rewards of today in your marriage or kids, your bank account, or your circumstances. Your gaze is fixed on the person and work of Christ and what matters for eternity. You live with hope and a future.

BENEDICTION

Even as you close this workbook, God's work in you is not finished. Take a moment to write a prayer for God to take all that you've learned and continue shaping your heart to be like his. Also, take time to pray for future generations that his Word at work in your heart and family will impact your children, your grandchildren, your great-grandchildren, and far beyond.

_____

_____

_____

_____

_____

_____

_____

_____

_____

I completed this workbook on:

_____ / _____ / _____